Thriving with PDA Autism for Teens

A Comprehensive Guide for Building Resilience, Managing Symptoms, and Achieving Independence

Lois Sutton

TABLE OF CONTENTS

INTRODUCTION

Welcome to "Thriving with PDA Autism for Teens," a comprehensive guide designed to support teenagers navigating the challenges of Pathological Demand Avoidance (PDA) Autism. In this intricate exploration, we delve into the intricacies of PDA Autism, offering insights, strategies, and tools to empower teens, their families, and support networks. As we embark on this journey, it is crucial to recognize the unique aspects of PDA Autism and the importance of tailored approaches for teens facing this neurodevelopmental condition.

Understanding PDA Autism

PDA Autism, or Pathological Demand Avoidance, represents a distinct profile within the autism spectrum. This chapter serves as a foundational exploration, unraveling the characteristics and traits that define PDA Autism. It goes beyond the conventional understanding of autism, emphasizing the nuanced nature of demand avoidance. Readers will gain insights into the challenges teens with PDA face, such as heightened anxiety, difficulties with transitions, and a pervasive need to control their environment.

The chapter delves into the sensory sensitivities and social communication struggles that often accompany PDA Autism. By fostering a deep understanding of these intricacies, readers can empathize with the unique experiences of teenagers with PDA. Through real-life examples and expert perspectives, we aim to dispel misconceptions and promote a nuanced understanding of PDA Autism.

Purpose and Scope of the Guide

The purpose of "Thriving with PDA Autism for Teens" is to empower teenagers, their families, educators, and caregivers with practical strategies for navigating the challenges associated with PDA Autism. This guide recognizes the multifaceted nature of PDA and seeks to provide a comprehensive resource for building resilience, managing symptoms, and achieving independence.

The scope of this guide extends beyond a mere compilation of information. It is a roadmap, offering practical tools and actionable advice. Whether you are a teenager striving for autonomy, a parent seeking guidance, or an educator working to create an inclusive environment, this guide is tailored to meet your needs. The insights provided are grounded in both research and lived experiences, ensuring a well-rounded and empathetic approach.

Readers will find a wealth of information on coping strategies, emotional regulation techniques, and behavioral interventions. Moreover, the guide addresses the intersection of PDA with educational settings, emphasizing the importance of understanding and accommodating the unique learning styles of teens with PDA Autism.

Chapter 1

Overview of PDA Autism

Understanding PDA Autism is a critical first step in providing effective support and guidance for individuals navigating this unique profile within the autism spectrum.

What is PDA Autism?

Pathological Demand Avoidance, commonly known as PDA Autism, is a distinctive subset within the broader autism spectrum. It is characterized by an intense need to resist and avoid the ordinary demands of daily life. Unlike traditional autism, individuals with PDA often display surface-level sociability and can appear more socially engaged. However, beneath this veneer lies a complex relationship with control, anxiety, and a pervasive resistance to imposed demands.

One hallmark feature of PDA Autism is the pathological avoidance of demands, which extends beyond typical avoidance behavior. Individuals with PDA may actively refuse or resist requests, exhibiting high levels of anxiety when faced with expectations. It is essential to recognize that demand avoidance is not merely a display of defiance but a coping mechanism rooted in anxiety and a need for control.

Unlike some forms of autism where social challenges are more overt, individuals with PDA may employ sophisticated social masking techniques. This involves mimicking social behaviors to fit in, making it challenging to identify their underlying struggles. Understanding the nuances of social masking is crucial for recognizing PDA in diverse social contexts and ensuring accurate diagnosis and support.

It is very important to note that PDA Autism often coexists with other conditions such as anxiety disorders, attention deficit hyperactivity disorder (ADHD), and sensory processing difficulties. Recognizing these overlapping traits is pivotal for a comprehensive understanding of the individual's neurodevelopmental profile.

Characteristics and Traits

Heightened Anxiety and Emotional Instability

A core feature of PDA Autism is the heightened levels of anxiety individuals experience, particularly in response to perceived demands. This anxiety can manifest as emotional meltdowns, intense reactions, or avoidance strategies. Understanding the emotional landscape of individuals with PDA is essential for creating supportive environments that mitigate stressors and foster emotional well-being.

Difficulties with Transitions and Unpredictability

Teens with PDA often struggle with transitions and unexpected changes in routine. The need for predictability and control is paramount, and disruptions can trigger anxiety and resistance. Exploring the reasons behind these difficulties provides valuable insights into the nature of demand avoidance and aids in crafting strategies to ease transitions for individuals with PDA.

Cognitive Flexibility Challenges

Individuals with PDA Autism may exhibit difficulties in cognitive flexibility, making it challenging for them to shift attention or adapt to new tasks. This difficulty contributes to inflexibility and makes them resistance to change.

Social Communication Complexities

While individuals with PDA may appear socially adept on the surface, closer examination reveals subtle differences in social communication. Some of these complexities associated with PDA, including difficulties in understanding social cues, maintaining reciprocal relationships, and navigating the unwritten rules of social interaction.

Diagnosis and Assessment

Clinical Evaluation and Observations

Accurate diagnosis of PDA Autism involves a comprehensive clinical evaluation, considering both behavioral observations and detailed interviews with parents, caregivers, and, if possible, the individual themselves.

Recognizing Early Signs and Indicators

Early recognition of potential signs of PDA is crucial for timely intervention which may include indicators, such as a typical demand avoidance behaviors, social difficulties, and anxiety-related responses. Understanding these early signs contributes to a proactive approach in seeking diagnostic assessments and support.

Collaboration with Multidisciplinary Teams

The diagnostic process for PDA Autism often involves collaboration among various professionals, including psychologists, speech therapists, occupational therapists, and educators. This interdisciplinary approach ensures a holistic understanding of the individual's strengths and challenges.

Differential Diagnosis and Coexisting Conditions

Distinguishing PDA from other conditions within the autism spectrum and related neurodevelopmental disorders is a very nuanced task. PDA may overlap with conditions like autism spectrum disorder (ASD), ADHD, and anxiety disorders, guiding clinicians are important in making accurate assessments.

It is essential to recognize that the diagnosis of PDA Autism is not a one-size-fits-all process. Each individual is unique, and the assessment should be tailored to the specific challenges and strengths of the person being evaluated. A multidisciplinary approach, involving psychologists, speech therapists, and occupational therapists, enhances the accuracy of the diagnosis and informs a comprehensive intervention plan.

Chapter 2

Navigating Teenhood with PDA

Navigating the tumultuous waters of adolescence is a challenge for any teenager, but for those with Pathological Demand Avoidance (PDA) Autism, the journey is often even more complex. Chapter 2 of "Thriving with PDA Autism for Teens" delves into the unique challenges and opportunities faced by teens with PDA during this critical stage of development. From the impact on social interactions to the nuances of educational considerations, this chapter aims to shed light on the multifaceted aspects of navigating teenhood with PDA.

Challenges and Opportunities

Teenhood is a period marked by numerous challenges and opportunities, and for individuals with PDA, these aspects take on a distinctive flavor. The inherent need for control and the avoidance of demands can present significant hurdles in various aspects of daily life. Teens with PDA often grapple with heightened anxiety, making social interactions, academic pursuits, and even routine tasks more challenging.

Navigating friendships can be particularly intricate for teens with PDA. While there might be a desire for social connection, the anxiety associated with social interactions can lead to difficulties in forming and maintaining friendships. Therefore the need for a delicate balance between the desire for social connection and the challenges posed by the need to avoid social demands.

The **academic landscape** is another arena where challenges and opportunities intertwine. The inherent difficulties with transitions, unpredictability, and resistance to demands can impact the learning environment. It is therefore important to highlight the potential strengths and talents that individuals with PDA may possess, such as creativity, problem-solving skills, and a unique perspective on tasks. Unraveling these complexities allows for a more nuanced understanding of the challenges teens with PDA face, while also recognizing the untapped potential that lies within.

Social interactions are a cornerstone of adolescent development, shaping one's sense of identity, belonging, and self-esteem. For teens with PDA, the impact on social interactions is profound and multifaceted. The unique blend of social masking and genuine struggles with social communication can create a dynamic where the external appearance may not align with internal experiences.

One notable challenge is the discrepancy between the apparent sociability of individuals with PDA and their internal struggles with social demands. While they may exhibit surface-level social skills, the underlying anxiety and need for control can result in complex and sometimes unpredictable social behaviors.

Friendships can become a source of both desire and distress for teens with PDA. The innate longing for connection clashes with the fear of demands inherent in maintaining friendships. This internal conflict can lead to social isolation or strained relationships. Exploring these dynamics is crucial for understanding the social challenges faced by teens with PDA and developing strategies to support healthy social development.

Moreover, the impact of social interactions extends beyond peer relationships to family dynamics. The need for control and resistance to demands can influence family dynamics, leading to potential conflicts and misunderstandings. This can be helped by emphasizing the importance of open communication, empathy, and a collaborative approach within the family unit.

In the **realm of education,** the challenges posed by PDA Autism require a thoughtful and tailored approach. Educational considerations for teens with PDA encompass a spectrum of factors, from classroom accommodations to understanding individual learning styles and strengths.

Teens with PDA may struggle with transitions between subjects or activities, resist following instructions, and experience heightened anxiety in response to academic demands. Understanding these challenges allows educators and parents to collaborate on implementing strategies that create a supportive and inclusive learning environment.

Individualized Education Programs (IEPs) become pivotal tools in addressing the unique needs of teens with PDA. Tailoring educational plans to accommodate the specific challenges associated with PDA ensures that teens receive the support necessary to thrive academically.

In addition to challenges, educational considerations also shine a light on the strengths and talents that teens with PDA may possess. Creative thinking, problem-solving skills, and a unique perspective can be valuable assets in the academic setting. Recognizing and fostering these strengths contributes to a holistic approach that acknowledges both the challenges and opportunities within the educational landscape.

Chapter 3

Building Resilience

Resilience is a vital aspect of thriving with PDA Autism, especially during the turbulent years of adolescence.

Coping Strategies for Stress

Coping with stress is an intricate dance for teens with PDA, whose heightened anxiety levels can make daily demands feel overwhelming.

One effective strategy is the implementation of structured routines. Establishing predictability in daily activities can offer a sense of control for individuals with PDA, reducing anxiety and enhancing their ability to manage stressors. It is therefore important to create and maintain consistent routines tailored to the individual's preferences and needs.

Another key coping strategy involves the use of relaxation techniques. Teens with PDA may benefit from mindfulness practices, deep breathing exercises, or sensory-based activities to help regulate their stress levels. Understanding the role of relaxation in stress management and incorporating these techniques into daily routines can contribute significantly to building resilience.

Furthermore, fostering effective communication is essential. Teens with PDA often face challenges in expressing their emotions and needs, leading to increased stress. Encourage open dialogue, ensuring that individuals with PDA feel heard and understood. Effective communication not only enhances self-expression but also facilitates the building of supportive relationships.

While structured routines provide a sense of security, flexibility allows for adaptation to changing circumstances. Finding a balance between structure and flexibility empowers teens with PDA to navigate the dynamic nature of daily life while minimizing stressors.

Additionally, exploring the concept of personal space as a coping strategy is crucial. Recognizing the need for alone time or a designated safe space provides individuals with PDA an opportunity to recharge and regroup during challenging moments. Creating and respecting these personal boundaries contributes to emotional well-being and resilience.

Emotional Regulation Techniques

Emotional regulation is a cornerstone of resilience, particularly for individuals with PDA who may experience intense emotions in response to various stimuli. This section of the chapter focuses on equipping teens with PDA with effective emotional regulation techniques to navigate the complex landscape of their emotions.

One essential technique is the development of emotional self-awareness. Teens with PDA benefit from recognizing and understanding their emotions, allowing them to navigate their internal experiences more effectively. Explore strategies for enhancing emotional self-awareness, such as journaling, self-reflection, and the use of visual aids to identify and articulate emotions.

Mindfulness practices emerge as powerful tools for emotional regulation. Techniques such as meditation, body scans, and grounding exercises can help individuals with PDA stay present in the moment and manage overwhelming emotions. Incorporating mindfulness into daily routines contributes to a more balanced emotional state and enhances overall well-being.

In addition to mindfulness, sensory regulation plays a pivotal role in emotional self-regulation for individuals with PDA. From creating sensory-friendly environments to incorporating sensory breaks, these techniques aim to provide individuals with PDA the tools they need to regulate their emotions effectively.

Social stories and visual supports also feature prominently in this section, offering a structured and visual way to understand and process emotions. Developing personalized social stories that address specific emotional situations empowers teens with PDA to navigate social and emotional complexities with greater ease.

Moreover, recognizing the connection between physical activity and emotional regulation is crucial. Engaging in regular physical exercise not only contributes to overall well-being but also serves as an outlet for pent-up energy and stress. Incorporating physical activities into daily routines highlights a positive impact on emotional resilience.

Developing a Support System

A robust support system is a cornerstone of resilience for individuals with PDA, providing the scaffolding necessary to navigate the challenges of adolescence.

Family support is foundational in this regard. Understanding the impact of PDA on family dynamics and fostering open communication are key components of family support. So the first step is creating a supportive family environment, including setting realistic expectations, promoting empathy, and encouraging collaborative problem-solving.

Peer relationships also play a crucial role in a teenager's support system. From structured social activities to communication skills development, these strategies aim to enhance the social support network for individuals with PDA.

Educational support forms another essential pillar of resilience. Collaborating with educators to create an inclusive and understanding school environment is pivotal.

Professional support, including mental health professionals and therapists, is explored as a valuable component of the support system. Therapeutic interventions, counseling, and specialized support services contribute to building emotional resilience and coping skills.

Community engagement is highlighted as an additional layer of support. Connecting with local autism communities, support groups, and advocacy organizations provides a broader network of understanding and assistance.

Chapter

Managing Syn

Managing the symptoms associated with Pathological Demand Avoidance (PDA) Autism is a nuanced process that requires a deep understanding of the unique challenges individuals face. Chapter 4 of "Thriving with PDA Autism for Teens" delves into three crucial aspects of symptom management: Sensory Sensitivities, Executive Function Challenges, and Behavioral Strategies. By addressing these components comprehensively, this chapter aims to equip teens, their families, and support networks with practical tools to navigate the complexities of PDA.

Sensory Sensitivities

Sensory sensitivities are a hallmark feature of PDA Autism, influencing how individuals perceive and respond to their environment.

Understanding the specific sensory triggers for individuals with PDA is crucial. This involves recognizing sensitivities to stimuli such as lights, sounds, textures, and smells. By identifying these triggers, individuals, their families, and caregivers can implement targeted strategies to create sensory-friendly environments. This may include using noise-canceling headphones, providing sensory-friendly clothing options, and utilizing soft lighting.

Moreover, developing a sensory diet tailored to the individual's needs is an essential component of managing sensory sensitivities. This involves incorporating activities that either stimulate or calm the senses based on the individual's preferences. Activities may include sensory breaks, tactile play, or the use of fidget tools.

Creating sensory-friendly spaces both at home and in educational settings is emphasized as a key strategy. This involves minimizing overwhelming stimuli and providing a designated safe space where individuals with PDA can retreat when sensory overload occurs.

Gradual exposure to sensory stimuli, combined with positive reinforcement, can help individuals with PDA build tolerance over time. Understanding the principles of desensitization and incorporating these techniques into daily routines contributes to the overall management of sensory sensitivities.

Executive Function Challenges

Executive function challenges present significant hurdles for individuals with PDA Autism, impacting various cognitive processes such as planning, organizing, initiating tasks, and shifting between activities.

Breaking tasks into manageable steps is a fundamental approach to address executive function challenges. This involves providing clear and concise instructions, creating visual schedules, and utilizing checklists. By simplifying tasks and providing structure, individuals with PDA can better navigate the demands of daily life.

Time management poses a particular challenge for individuals with PDA, often leading to difficulties in punctuality and planning. In respect to this, explore techniques for improving time awareness, including the use of visual timers, alarms, and scheduling tools. These tools serve as external supports to compensate for internal challenges in time perception.

Organization skills are another focal point in addressing executive function challenges. This section explores the benefits of creating organized and clutter-free spaces, implementing systems for managing belongings, and developing routines to streamline daily activities. The goal is to reduce cognitive load and enhance the individual's ability to initiate and complete tasks successfully.

Furthermore, fostering self-regulation is essential in managing executive function challenges. This involves teaching individuals with PDA to recognize and regulate their emotions, particularly those related to frustration and overwhelm. Delve into strategies such as mindfulness, deep breathing exercises, and self-reflection to promote emotional self-regulation in the face of executive function challenges.

Collaboration with educators and the implementation of accommodations in educational settings are explored as key components of managing executive function challenges. This includes the development of Individualized Education Programs (IEPs) that address the specific executive function needs of individuals with PDA

.

Behavioral Strategies

Behavioral strategies play a pivotal role in managing the symptoms associated with PDA Autism, providing a framework for understanding and responding to challenging behaviors.

Understanding the function of behavior is a fundamental concept in behavioral strategies. Challenging behaviors often serve as a means of communication or a way to cope with overwhelming demands. By identifying the underlying function of behaviors, caregivers and educators can develop targeted interventions to address the root causes.

Developing clear and consistent expectations is crucial in managing challenging behaviors. This involves establishing predictable routines, setting realistic goals, and providing clear communication about expectations.

The use of visual supports emerges as a valuable tool in behavioral strategies. Visual schedules, social stories, and visual cues provide individuals with PDA a concrete and structured way to understand expectations and navigate social situations.

Addressing meltdowns and other intense behaviors is a significant aspect of behavioral strategies. This involves developing strategies to de-escalate situations, provide sensory comfort, and teach alternative coping mechanisms. This may include techniques such as planned ignoring, redirection, and sensory interventions to manage and prevent meltdowns effectively.

Moreover, collaborative problem-solving is emphasized as a proactive approach to behavioral challenges. Involving individuals with PDA in the decision-making process and providing choices within a structured framework empower them to exert control in a positive manner.

In educational settings, collaboration between parents, educators, and specialists is pivotal in implementing behavioral strategies. The development of Behavioral Intervention Plans (BIPs) within the framework of

Individualized Education Programs (IEPs) allows for a cohesive and coordinated approach. The chapter highlights the importance of consistent communication and collaboration to ensure that behavioral strategies are implemented effectively across various settings.

Chapter 5

Achieving Independence

Independence is a crucial aspect of the developmental journey for teenagers, and for those with Pathological Demand Avoidance (PDA) Autism, achieving autonomy requires a tailored approach. Chapter 5, "Achieving Independence," delves into three pivotal dimensions: Life Skills for Teens with PDA, Transitioning to Adulthood, and Vocational and Educational Planning. This chapter aims to provide comprehensive insights and practical strategies to empower teens with PDA on their path toward independence.

Life Skills for Teens with PDA

Navigating the complexities of daily life requires a foundation of essential life skills. For teens with PDA, developing these skills takes on added significance due to the unique challenges associated with the condition.

One fundamental aspect is self-care, encompassing activities such as personal hygiene, dressing, and meal preparation. Developing routines and breaking down these tasks into manageable steps assists teens with PDA in acquiring and refining self-care skills.

Time management is another critical life skill that plays a role in achieving independence. Teens with PDA often struggle with time perception and organization. Introducing tools such as visual schedules, timers, and planners aids in enhancing time management skills.

Furthermore, social skills form an integral component of achieving independence. Building and maintaining relationships, navigating social situations, and understanding social cues are vital aspects of social competence. Targeted strategies such as social stories, role-playing, and peer modeling to support the development of social skills for teens with PDA.

Problem-solving and decision-making skills are emphasized as essential for navigating the challenges of daily life. Teaching teens with PDA to analyze situations, consider consequences, and make informed choices contributes to their ability to navigate various scenarios independently.

In addition, fostering a sense of responsibility for personal belongings and managing personal space contributes to the development of independence. Implementing organizational strategies, such as designated spaces for belongings and checklists, empowers teens with PDA to take ownership of their environment.

Transitioning to Adulthood

Transitioning from adolescence to adulthood is a pivotal phase, and for individuals with PDA, this journey involves unique considerations. This section of the chapter explores the challenges and opportunities associated with transitioning to adulthood, offering guidance for individuals, families, and support networks.

One primary focus is the transition from pediatric to adult healthcare services. Understanding the changes in healthcare support and advocating for a seamless transition is essential. Individuals with PDA should be prepared for healthcare autonomy, including self-advocacy skills and building a collaborative relationship with healthcare providers.

Developing independence in daily living skills becomes increasingly significant during the transition to adulthood. During this time the process of fostering autonomy in areas such as cooking, cleaning, and managing finances helps develop independence. Practical strategies, including hands-on learning experiences and gradual independence-building, are explored to support teens with PDA in developing crucial life skills.

Educational transitions mark another key aspect of the journey to adulthood. This includes the shift from secondary education to post-secondary options or vocational training. Understanding the options available and collaboratively planning educational transitions ensures that individuals with PDA receive the support necessary to pursue their goals.

Moreover, addressing emotional and mental health considerations during the transition to adulthood is paramount. Teens with PDA may experience heightened anxiety about the uncertainties associated with adulthood. At this time, it is important to develop emotional resilience, self-regulation, and coping skills to navigate the emotional landscape of the transition to adulthood.

Building independence in decision-making and self-advocacy is a central theme during the transition to adulthood. This involves empowering teens with PDA to actively participate in decision-making processes, express their preferences, and advocate for their needs. This can be done by developing decision-making frameworks and teaching self-advocacy skills, to enhance independence in decisional autonomy.

Vocational and Educational Planning

The intersection of vocational and educational planning plays a pivotal role in shaping the trajectory of individuals with PDA as they transition to adulthood.

Identifying strengths, interests, and preferences is a foundational step in vocational planning. Understanding the individual's abilities and inclinations guides the exploration of potential career paths. Assessments, vocational testing, and career exploration in identifying suitable vocational options for teens with PDA is practiced.

Developing practical vocational skills is integral to vocational planning. This involves providing opportunities for hands-on experiences, internships, and vocational training.

Collaboration with vocational counselors and educators becomes pivotal in the vocational planning process. This includes developing Individualized Education Programs (IEPs) that integrate vocational goals and support services.

Chapter 6

Family Dynamics and Support

Family dynamics play a central role in the journey of individuals with Pathological Demand Avoidance (PDA) Autism, influencing their support networks and overall well-being. Chapter 6, "Family Dynamics and Support," delves into three critical dimensions: Understanding Family Roles, Communication Strategies, and Resources for Families. This chapter aims to provide insights and practical guidance for families of individuals with PDA, fostering understanding, effective communication, and the utilization of available resources to navigate the unique challenges associated with PDA.

Understanding Family Roles

The dynamics within a family profoundly impact the experiences of individuals with PDA, shaping their environment and support systems. Understanding family roles is crucial for fostering a supportive and empathetic atmosphere.

The role of parents is multifaceted, encompassing advocacy, emotional support, and guidance. Parents of individuals with PDA often find themselves navigating complex challenges, from managing demanding behaviors to coordinating educational and therapeutic interventions. Understanding the unique needs of their child and adopting a collaborative and informed approach becomes essential. Also the role of parents in balance support and boundaries, recognizing the importance of self-care in sustaining their ability to advocate effectively.

Siblings play a significant role in the family dynamic, and their experiences warrant attention. Siblings of individuals with PDA may navigate a range of emotions, from understanding and empathy to frustration and confusion. Fostering open communication and providing age-appropriate information about PDA contribute to creating an inclusive family environment. For individuals with PDA, positive sibling relationships, fostering a sense of understanding and collaboration is very paramount.

Extended family members can also play key roles in providing support. Grandparents, aunts, uncles, and cousins may contribute to the overall support network. Educating extended family members about PDA, clarifying misconceptions, and encouraging their involvement can enhance the breadth of support available. Creating a united front within the extended family, ensuring that individuals with PDA receive consistent understanding and support.

Moreover, recognizing the impact of PDA on family roles and dynamics is pivotal. This involves acknowledging the potential strains on family relationships and working collaboratively to address challenges. Fostering a sense of unity and resilience within the family unit is essential for creating a supportive environment for individuals with PDA.

Communication Strategies

Effective communication within a family is a cornerstone of understanding and support for individuals with PDA. Navigating the communication challenges associated with PDA requires adopting strategies that foster clarity, empathy, and mutual understanding. Clear and consistent communication is foundational. Individuals with PDA may struggle with interpreting ambiguous language or implied meanings. Using clear instructions, avoiding ambiguous language, and providing visual supports contribute to creating a communication environment that aligns with the preferences and needs of individuals with PDA.

Active listening is a skill that enhances communication within the family. This involves giving full attention, asking clarifying questions, and validating the experiences and emotions of individuals with PDA. Cultivating a habit of active listening fosters a deeper understanding of the perspectives and needs of individuals with PDA.

Visual supports emerge as powerful tools in facilitating communication. Visual schedules, social stories, and visual cues provide concrete and structured ways to convey information. Using visual supports helps individuals with PDA anticipate and understand expectations, reducing anxiety and enhancing communication.

Creating a communication-friendly environment involves minimizing sensory distractions and optimizing conditions for effective interaction. Establishing routines for family communication, incorporating sensory-friendly elements, and considering individual preferences contribute to a communication environment that aligns with the needs of individuals with PDA.

Additionally, recognizing the role of nonverbal communication is essential. Individuals with PDA may struggle with interpreting subtle facial expressions, body language, and tone of voice. Nonverbal communication within the family, emphasizing the use of clear gestures, facial expressions, and tone to convey messages can be effective. Fostering a communication style that aligns with the preferences of individuals with PDA contributes to a more harmonious family dynamic.

Furthermore, incorporating technology as a communication tool can be beneficial. Social communication apps, visual schedules on electronic devices, and online resources can enhance communication and information sharing within the family. The advantages of incorporating technology to support communication, provides families with additional tools to facilitate understanding and connection.

Resources for Families

Accessing appropriate resources is fundamental for families navigating the challenges associated with PDA. This section of the chapter explores the array of resources available to support families, including educational materials, support groups, therapeutic interventions, and advocacy organizations.

Educational materials play a crucial role in equipping families with the knowledge and tools to understand and support individuals with PDA. Books, articles, and online resources provide valuable insights into the characteristics of PDA, strategies for managing symptoms, and fostering resilience. Explore recommended educational materials, offering families a curated list of resources to deepen their understanding of PDA.

Support groups offer a sense of community and shared experiences for families facing similar challenges. Online and in-person support groups provide opportunities for families to connect, share insights, and receive emotional support.

Chapter 7

School and Community Involvement

Navigating the educational landscape and community interactions are pivotal aspects of the journey for individuals with Pathological Demand Avoidance (PDA) Autism. Chapter 7, "School and Community Involvement," delves into three crucial dimensions: Advocating for Educational Needs, Building Positive Relationships, and Community Engagement. This chapter aims to provide comprehensive insights and practical strategies for families and individuals with PDA to actively participate in the school environment and engage with the broader community.

Advocating for Educational Needs

Advocating for the educational needs of individuals with PDA is a dynamic and ongoing process that involves collaboration between families, educators, and support professionals.

Understanding the educational rights of individuals with PDA is foundational to effective advocacy. Familiarity with laws such as the Individuals with Disabilities Education Act (IDEA) and Section 504 of the Rehabilitation Act empowers families to advocate for appropriate accommodations and services. This section provides an overview of relevant legislation and highlights key components that impact the educational rights of individuals with PDA.

Developing a collaborative relationship with educators is essential for successful advocacy. Open communication, regular updates on the individual's progress, and sharing insights about PDA contribute to a supportive educational environment. This is to foster a sense of partnership in meeting the educational needs of individuals with PDA.

Moreover, advocating for social and emotional support within the school setting is paramount. This involves addressing the unique social challenges individuals with PDA may face and incorporating strategies for social skills development.

The process of advocating for educational needs extends beyond the individual classroom to include broader educational environments. Developing transition plans, fostering collaboration between educators, and ensuring continuity of support contribute to a smoother educational journey for individuals with PDA.

Building Positive Relationships

Positive relationships within the school community are instrumental in creating an inclusive and supportive environment for individuals with PDA. Fostering understanding among peers is a key aspect of building positive relationships within the school environment. This involves implementing strategies to raise awareness about PDA, promoting empathy, and encouraging inclusive practices. Building positive relationships with teachers is essential for creating a supportive educational experience. Educators who understand the unique needs of individuals with PDA can tailor their teaching strategies and provide effective support.

Creating a positive rapport with school staff and administrators is crucial for addressing the broader support needs of individuals with PDA. This involves building relationships with special education coordinators, school counselors, and other professionals who play a role in supporting the individual's educational journey.

Community Engagement

Engaging with the broader community is a valuable aspect of the social and developmental journey for individuals with PDA. Participating in community activities and events offers opportunities for individuals with PDA to develop social skills and build connections. From sports programs to art classes, finding community-based activities enhances the social and recreational experiences of individuals with PDA.

Creating a supportive network within the local community involves educating others about PDA. From organizing community workshops to collaborating with local organizations, families can play a proactive role in creating an informed and inclusive community environment.

Accessing community resources and support services is a key aspect of community engagement for families of individuals with PDA. Establishing connections with community resources enhances the overall support network available to families and individuals with PDA. Promoting inclusivity within the community involves fostering understanding among neighbors, classmates, and local businesses. Creating a community that values diversity and supports individuals with PDA contributes to a more enriching and accepting social environment. Moreover, community engagement includes advocating for accessibility and accommodation. This involves working with local organizations, businesses, and public spaces to ensure that individuals with PDA can participate fully in community activities.

Chapter 8

Self-Advocacy

Self-advocacy is a transformative skill that empowers individuals with Pathological Demand Avoidance (PDA) Autism to navigate various aspects of their lives with agency and resilience. Chapter 8, "Self-Advocacy," delves into three critical dimensions: Empowering Teens with PDA, Communicating Needs Effectively, and Advocacy in Various Settings. This chapter aims to provide comprehensive insights and practical strategies for teens with PDA to develop and exercise their self-advocacy skills in a variety of contexts.

Empowering Teens with PDA

Empowering teens with PDA is foundational to the development of self-advocacy skills. This is to explore strategies and principles for fostering a sense of empowerment, self-awareness, and confidence in teens with PDA.

Recognizing and celebrating individual strengths is a key component of empowerment. This involves identifying and acknowledging the unique talents, interests, and abilities of teens with PDA. This is important when cultivating a positive self-image, encouraging teens to recognize and take pride in their strengths, and building a foundation of self-confidence.

Fostering self-awareness is essential for teens with PDA to navigate their strengths and challenges effectively. Encouraging teens to understand their sensory sensitivities, communication preferences, and stress triggers empowers them to communicate their needs more effectively in various settings.

Encouraging autonomy in decision-making contributes to the empowerment of teens with PDA. This involves providing opportunities for teens to make choices, express preferences, and actively participate in decisional processes.

Moreover, promoting self-determination is a central aspect of empowering teens with PDA. Encourage them to set goals, express aspirations, and actively participate in shaping their future. Fostering a sense of agency and ownership over one's life contributes to the development of a resilient and self-advocating mindset.

Creating a supportive environment that values and respects the perspectives of teens with PDA is paramount. This involves fostering open communication, active listening, and a collaborative approach within the family and support network. Encourage building a foundation of trust, respect, and understanding that enables teens with PDA to express their needs and preferences confidently.

Communicating Needs Effectively

Promoting self-regulation in communication is essential for individuals with PDA, particularly in situations that may elicit stress or anxiety. This involves developing strategies to manage emotions, stay composed, and communicate needs effectively even in challenging situations. explore techniques such as deep breathing, mindfulness, and self-reflection to enhance self-regulation in communication.

Advocacy in Various Settings

Self-advocacy is a dynamic skill that individuals with PDA can apply in a variety of settings, from educational environments to healthcare settings and beyond. Advocating for educational needs is a central aspect of self-advocacy for individuals with PDA. This involves actively participating in the Individualized Education Program (IEP) process, expressing preferences for accommodations, and collaborating with educators to create a supportive learning environment.

Promoting self-advocacy in healthcare settings is essential for individuals with PDA to receive personalized and respectful care. Encouraging teens with PDA to actively participate in healthcare decisions and self-advocate for their well-being is pivotal for a positive healthcare experience. Navigating social settings requires individuals with PDA to apply their self-advocacy skills to communicate effectively with peers, family members, and community members. Fostering a sense of agency in social settings contributes to a more enriching and inclusive social experience.

Advocating for employment and vocational goals is a critical aspect of self-advocacy for individuals with PDA transitioning to adulthood. This involves expressing preferences for workplace accommodations, communicating strengths and challenges, and actively participating in vocational planning. Building self-advocacy skills in the community involves navigating public spaces, engaging with local organizations, and expressing needs in various settings. Empowering individuals with PDA to navigate and contribute to the community enhances their overall sense of agency and belonging.

CONCLUSION

The journey of thriving with PDA Autism for teens is multifaceted, encompassing a myriad of challenges, triumphs, and growth opportunities. Throughout this comprehensive guide, we've explored the intricacies of PDA Autism, delving into strategies for building resilience, managing symptoms, achieving independence, navigating school and community involvement, fostering family dynamics, and developing crucial self-advocacy skills. As we reach the conclusion of this guide, it's essential to reflect on the key themes and insights that underpin the holistic approach advocated for individuals with PDA.

The future holds promise for advancements in understanding neurodiversity, refining diagnostic criteria, and developing targeted interventions. It is a collective responsibility to advocate for inclusivity, acceptance, and support structures that empower individuals with PDA to lead fulfilling lives.

In Closing

"Thriving with PDA Autism for Teens" is not just a guide; it is a testament to the resilience, strength, and potential of individuals with PDA. It serves as a compass for families, educators, and support networks, providing insights, strategies, and a roadmap for navigating the complexities of PDA. As we conclude this journey, may it be a source of inspiration and empowerment for all those touched by PDA, guiding them towards a future where individuals with PDA not only thrive but actively contribute to a more inclusive and understanding society.

Made in the USA
Monee, IL
18 March 2024